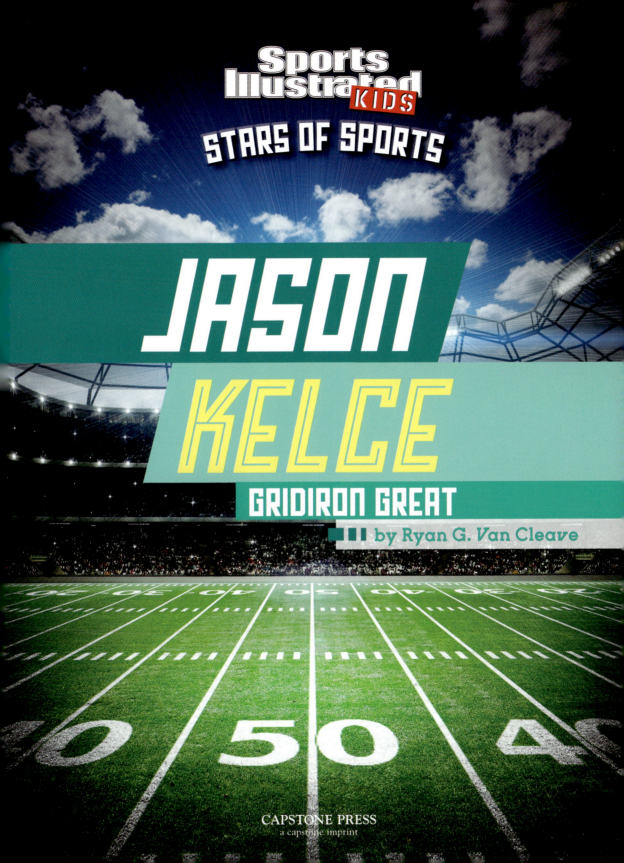

Sports Illustrated KID$

STARS OF SPORTS

JASON KELCE

GRIDIRON GREAT

by Ryan G. Van Cleave

CAPSTONE PRESS
a capstone imprint

Published by Capstone Press, an imprint of Capstone
1710 Roe Crest Drive, North Mankato, Minnesota 56003
capstonepub.com

Library of Congress Cataloging-in-Publication Data
Names: Van Cleave, Ryan G., 1972- author.
Title: Jason Kelce : gridiron great / Ryan G. Van Cleave.
Description: North Mankato, Minnesota : Capstone Press, [2025]
Series: Sports illustrated kids stars of sports | Includes bibliographical references and index.
Audience: Ages 8-11 | Audience: Grades 4-6
Summary: "Jason Kelce was a walk-on player for the University of Cincinnati Bearcats football team, where he played multiple positions. He was selected by the Philadelphia Eagles in the sixth round of the 2011 NFL Draft. Kelce wasn't as big as most centers, but he was fast and determined. His incredible work ethic and heartfelt passion have made Kelce a legend on and off the football field. Follow his inspirational path to becoming an NFL great"-- Provided by publisher.
Identifiers: LCCN 2024010294 (print) | LCCN 2024010295 (ebook) | ISBN 9781669094234 (hardcover) | ISBN 9781669094180 (paperback) | ISBN 9781669094197 (pdf) | ISBN 9781669094210 (kindle edition) | ISBN 9781669094203 (epub)
Subjects: LCSH: Kelce, Jason, 1987---Juvenile literature. | Football players--United States--Biography--Juvenile literature.
Classification: LCC GV939.K359 V36 2025 (print) | LCC GV939.K359 (ebook) | DDC 796.33209 [B]--dc23/eng/20240403
LC record available at https://lccn.loc.gov/2024010294
LC ebook record available at https://lccn.loc.gov/2024010295

Editorial Credits
Editor: Christianne Jones; Designer: Jaime Willems; Media Researcher: Svetlana Zhurkin; Production Specialist: Whitney Schaefer

Image Credits
Associated Press: Alex Brandon, 20, Chris Szagola, 25, Tom DiPace, cover, Tony Gutierrez, 17; Getty Images: Christian Petersen, 21, Cooper Neill, 23, Gregory Shamus, 19, Kevin Sabitus, 28, Mark Brown, 24, Mike Ehrmann, 5, NurPhoto/Bastiaan Slabbers, 9, Prime Video/Lisa Lake, 7, 27, Rich Schultz, 15; Newscom: Abaca USA/MCT/Yong Kim, 16, Cal Sport Media/Alan Schwartz, 13, Icon SMI AXA/John Korduner, 12, Icon SMI/Jim Owens, 11, Icon Sportswire/Andy Lewis, 22, Icon Sportswire/Robin Alam, 18; Shutterstock: Chad Robertson Media, 10, EFKS, 1

Source Notes
Page 5, "No one likes us . . ." Nick Piccone, "The Transcript of Jason Kelce's speech," *Philly Influencer*, February 9, 2018, https://phillyinfluencer.com/2018/02/the-transcript-of-jason-kelces-speech, Accessed January 16, 2024.

Page 7, "I picked him up . . ." Miranda Siwak, "Travis Kelce and Jason Kelce's Most Supportive Quotes About Each Other," *US Magazine*, November 20, 2023, https://www.usmagazine.com/celebrity-news/news/travis-kelce-and-jason-kelces-brotherly-bond-in-their-own-words, Accessed January 16, 2024.

Page 22, "Go celebrate . . ." Jordan Mendoza, "Travis and Jason Kelce hug after Super Bowl 57, embrace mom Donna," *USA Today*, February 12, 2023, https://www.usatoday.com/story/sports/nfl/super-bowl/2023/02/12/kelce-brothers-mom-share-emotional-embraces-after-super-bowl-57/11246405002, Accessed January 16, 2024.

Page 28, "It has always been a goal of mine . . ." Matt Mullin and Nick Vadala, "Jason Kelce's Retirement Speech, Annotated and Explained," *Philadelphia Inquirer*, March 6, 2024, https://www.inquirer.com/eagles/inq2/jason-kelce-retirement-speech-transcript-annotated-explained-20240306.html, Accessed March 12, 2024.

TABLE OF CONTENTS

Words in **BOLD** are in the glossary.

THE UNDERDOGS

Under the bright lights of U.S. Bank Stadium in Minneapolis, tension filled the air. It was Super Bowl LII. The Philadelphia Eagles faced the New England Patriots. The Eagles' starting quarterback was hurt. The team was led by backup quarterback Nick Foles. Legendary quarterback Tom Brady led the Patriots.

Despite the odds, the Eagles and their superstar center, Jason Kelce, played a relentless game. As the final whistle blew, the stadium erupted. The Eagles had clinched their first Super Bowl victory with a score of 41–33.

Days later, the city of Philadelphia celebrated. Wearing a colorful **mummer** costume, Kelce gave a memorable speech. He spoke from his heart to thousands of fans.

>>> Kelce sprints onto the field after winning the Super Bowl in 2018.

His words echoed the grit and spirit of the city: "No one likes us, we don't care!" This wasn't just a victory speech. It was a chant of triumph for every underdog who ever dared to dream big.

CHAPTER ONE

CLEVELAND HEIGHTS

Jason Kelce's journey to National Football League (NFL) stardom began in Cleveland Heights, Ohio. He was born on November 5, 1987. His father, Ed, worked in the sales industry. His mother, Donna, was a banking professional. Jason and his younger brother, Travis, grew up in a household where sports and competition were a way of life.

The two brothers had a lot of energy and played rough. A ball smashed through the family car's windshield. The garage door was dented from hockey slap shots. After an especially rough basketball game, they really got into it.

"I picked him up and threw him onto the kitchen floor," Travis said, "and knocked the stove off its hinges and everything." During that fight, their dad almost got hurt. From that point on, the brothers quit brawling. They channeled their aggression into sports instead.

>>> Donna and Jason were all smiles at the premiere of *Kelce* in 2023.

At Cleveland Heights High School, Kelce stood out in hockey and lacrosse. However, his heart belonged to football. He played on both sides of the ball. He was a running back and a linebacker. He was team captain his senior year.

Kelce's talents weren't limited to sports. He worked hard to balance sports and academics. He was also involved in music. Kelce played baritone saxophone in the school's jazz band.

These **formative** years at Cleveland Heights sculpted his character. The toughness, dedication, and balance he developed stuck with him.

Music Man

Kelce still plays the baritone saxophone. After winning the Super Bowl, Kelce joined the Philadelphia Orchestra to play "Fly Eagles Fly." He added vocals to two Christmas albums with teammates as well.

>>> In 2018, Kelce played saxophone with high school students in Philadelphia.

CHAPTER TWO

UNIVERSITY OF CINCINNATI

Despite Kelce's athletic talent, college **scouts** looked past him. His arrival at the University of Cincinnati marked the start of an unexpected journey.

As a **walk-on**, he didn't have the security of a scholarship player. Every practice and every game were a chance to prove he belonged. His determination earned him a scholarship.

〉〉〉 Kelce attended the University of Cincinnati from 2006 to 2010.

>>> Kelce protects his quarterback during a college game in 2009.

Kelce was a running back in high school. His path took a turn when coaches moved him to fullback. From there, he moved to the offensive line. This was a big change. Being on the offensive line required a different skill set. Kelce dove into learning new techniques and strategies.

Kelce's adaptability was impressive. He played left guard and center for three seasons as a Bearcat. His move to full-time center was the final piece in his college football journey. This was a role in which he truly excelled. He learned to spot defensive **schemes** and quickly alert teammates on how they should adjust.

FACT

Jason's brother, Travis, followed him to the University of Cincinnati. They played together during the 2009 season.

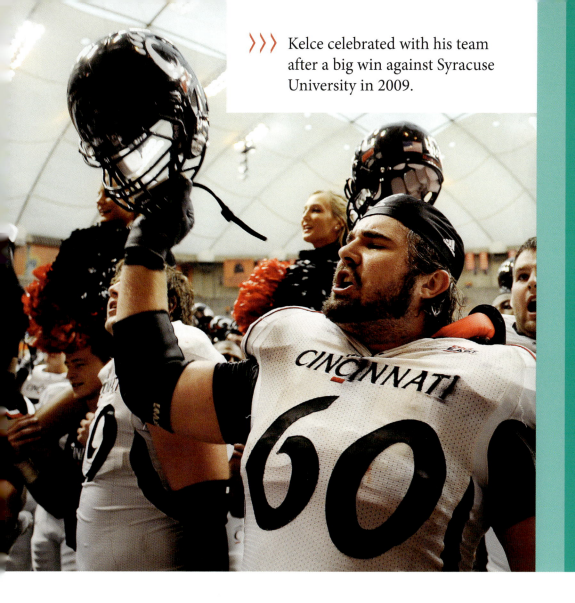

〉〉〉 Kelce celebrated with his team after a big win against Syracuse University in 2009.

Kelce was a two-time second-team All-Big East selection and an honorable mention All-American. He worked hard in school and was named first-team Academic All-American as well. During his time with the Bearcats, he played in three bowl games.

CHAPTER THREE

LIFE IN THE NFL

In 2011, Kelce's NFL dream came true. The Philadelphia Eagles chose him in the sixth round of the **draft**. He was undersized for an offensive lineman at 6 feet, 3 inches (191 centimeters) and 280 pounds (127 kilograms). But that didn't matter.

Kelce worked hard to prove himself, and it paid off. He earned a spot as the starting center on the Eagles' offensive line in his **rookie** season. His coaches and teammates were impressed by how much he knew about football and how hard he worked. He also became a team favorite with his lumberjack beard, easygoing charm, and goofy sense of humor.

FACT

At the 2011 NFL Scouting Combine, Kelce ran the fastest 40-yard dash of all offensive linemen. He did it in 4.89 seconds.

››› Kelce is known for his low stance and quick snap at center.

>>> Kelce leaving the field with a season-ending knee injury

Things weren't always easy. In 2012, Kelce injured his knee. It was a serious setback. But Kelce came back stronger and more determined than ever.

During his early years with the Eagles, Kelce's skills and leadership quickly became apparent. He was honored with the 2013 Ed Block Courage Award. The award showcased his resilience and character. His performance on the field earned him high grades from Pro Football Focus. It rated him as the best center in the NFL in 2013.

These early honors and his rapidly growing reputation as a leading center set the stage for his future successes.

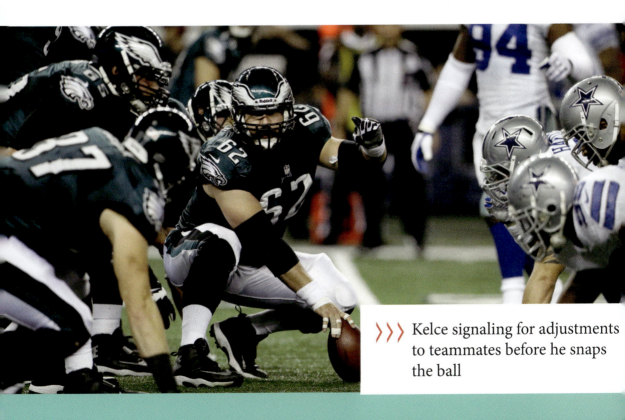

〉〉〉 Kelce signaling for adjustments to teammates before he snaps the ball

CHAPTER FOUR

SUPER BOWL GLORY

Super Bowl LII marked a **pivotal** moment in Kelce's NFL career. The season was full of challenges, including injuries to key players. Kelce's leadership and dependability were key. His masterful play as a center was crucial. He strengthened the Eagles' offense through each game leading up to the championship.

>>> Kelce working against a defensive end during a game

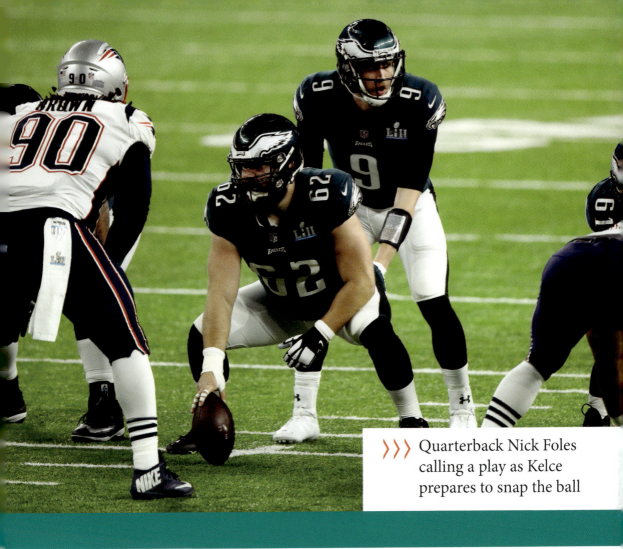

>>> Quarterback Nick Foles calling a play as Kelce prepares to snap the ball

The Super Bowl win showcased the team's determined spirit and unity. And Kelce's stellar performance was at the center of it all. His skills in reading defenses and anchoring the offensive line made all the difference.

>>> Kelce giving his inspiring Super Bowl victory speech

However, it was Kelce's passionate speech during the victory parade that captured the spirit of the Eagles' journey. His words **resonated** with emotion, pride, and a deep connection with Philadelphia. He's known as "The King of Philly" for good reason.

That wasn't Kelce's last chance to play in the Super Bowl. In 2023, the Eagles reached that goal again. This time, they would face the Kansas City Chiefs. Travis Kelce was a tight end for the Chiefs. For the first time ever, brothers would play against each other in the Super Bowl. As the National Anthem played, tears streamed down both brothers' faces.

FACT

Donna Kelce wore a custom half-and-half jersey for the game. The back represented the Eagles for Jason, and the front represented the Chiefs for Travis.

The game went back and forth all four quarters. The Eagles, with Kelce as their cornerstone, battled fiercely. But the Chiefs came out on top. The game ended in a nail-biting 38–35 loss for the Eagles. Though it hurt to be beaten by his little brother, Jason hugged him and said, "Go celebrate. I love you."

>>> Kelce blocking for a running back during the Super Bowl

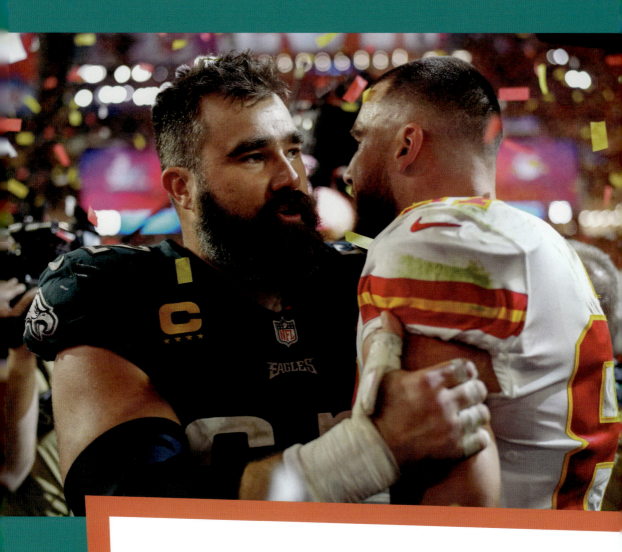

The Big Brother

Andy Reid coached the Philadelphia Eagles from 1999 to 2012. He drafted Jason. In 2013, Reid left Philadelphia and started coaching the Kansas City Chiefs. He wasn't sure about drafting Travis. But after a phone conversation with Jason, Reid was convinced. Travis credits his entire football career to his big brother.

CHAPTER FIVE

FUTURE BEYOND FOOTBALL

At age 36, Kelce played for 13 years. He started 193 games in a row. He has seven Pro Bowl selections and six First Team All-Pro honors. Without a doubt, those are Hall of Fame **credentials**.

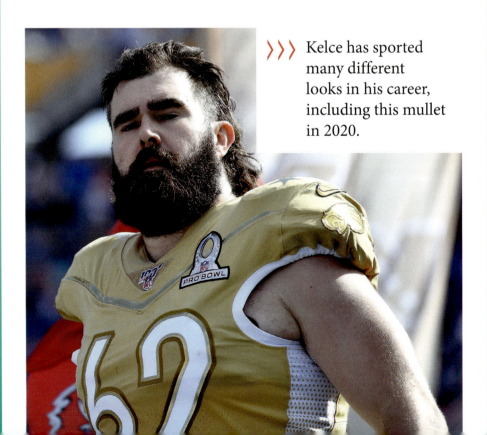

〉〉〉 Kelce has sported many different looks in his career, including this mullet in 2020.

>>> Kelce greeting fans in 2023

Kelce's life extends beyond football. He is a dedicated supporter of the Eagles Autism Foundation. In 2024, he even participated in a 5K Run/Walk.

In 2022, he launched the Underdog Apparel line. These locally produced, gender-neutral clothes celebrate the underdog spirit of Philadelphia. All profits go to Kelce's (Be)Philly Foundation. This nonprofit organization supports Philadelphia public school students.

It is clear that family is central to Kelce's life. He shares a strong bond with his superstar brother. They cohost the popular *New Heights* podcast. They talk about a range of topics including life, football, and personal experiences. His wife, Kylie, is a lifelong Eagles fan. The couple has three daughters.

Kelce wasn't born in Philadelphia, but the city loves him. He represents the true spirit of the city. He is strong, kind, and full of heart.

In 2024, Kelce announced his retirement during an emotional press conference. His mom, dad, brother, and wife were sitting in the front row, supporting him.

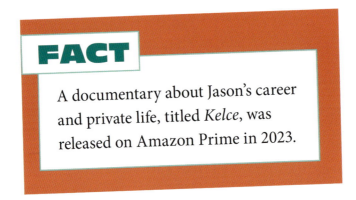

FACT

A documentary about Jason's career and private life, titled *Kelce*, was released on Amazon Prime in 2023.

>>> Jason and Kylie at the premiere of the *Kelce* documentary

"It has always been a goal of mine to play my whole career in one city, and I couldn't have dreamt of a better one, and a better fit, if I tried. I don't know what's next, but I look forward to the new challenges and opportunities that await, and I know that I carry with me the lessons from my time here, and that forever, we shall all share the bond of being Philadelphians. That's all I got."

〉〉〉 Kelce showing focus during one of his final games

TIMELINE

1987 Born November 5 in Cleveland Heights, Ohio

2006 Graduates from Cleveland Heights High School

2006 Joins the University of Cincinnati Bearcats football team as a walk-on; redshirts first year

2007 Plays left guard and center in nine college football games

2009 Both Kelce brothers play on the Bearcats football team

2009 Earns second-team All-Big East honors after starting 13 games at left guard

2010 Moves to center full time; named Honorable Mention All-American and second-team All-Big East

2011 Drafted by the Philadelphia Eagles

2011 Earns starting center position in his rookie season

2012 Endures a significant knee injury

2014 Selected to his first Pro Bowl (with six more selections since)

2018 Wins Super Bowl LII

2022 Launches *New Heights* podcast with his brother

2023 Plays in Super Bowl against his brother, losing 38–35

2023 Releases *Kelce* documentary

2023 Breaks the Eagles record for most consecutive starts

2024 Retires after 13 seasons with the Eagles

GLOSSARY

CREDENTIALS (kri-DEN-shuhlz)—in sports, a player's or coach's past achievements and experience

DRAFT (DRAFT)—process of selecting new players to join a professional sports team

FORMATIVE (FOR-muh-tiv)—relating to someone's early development or experiences

MUMMER (MUH-muhr)—a costumed performer

PIVOTAL (PIH-vuh-tuhl)—extremely important, often changing the direction of something

RESONATE (REH-suh-nayt)—a strong effect or impact on people

ROOKIE (RUH-kee)—first-year player in a professional sports league

SCHEMES (SKEEMZ)—plans or programs of action

SCOUTS (SKOWTS)—people who search for and identify talent, especially in sports

WALK-ON (WOK-on)—athlete who joins a team without first being recruited or receiving a scholarship

READ MORE

Anderson, Josh. *Inside the Philadelphia Eagles*. Minneapolis: Lerner, 2024.

Blue, Tyler. *Stars of the NFL*. New York: Abbeville Kids, 2023.

Smith, Elliott. *Courage on the Football Field and Other Football Skills*. North Mankato, MN: Capstone, 2021.

INTERNET SITES

(Be)Philly
bephilly.org/about

Facts.net: 16 Extraordinary Facts About Jason Kelce
facts.net/celebrity/16-extraordinary-facts-about-jason-kelce

Philadelphia Eagles: Jason Kelce
philadelphiaeagles.com/team/players-roster/jason-kelce

INDEX

AUTHOR BIO

Ryan G. Van Cleave is the author of dozens of books for children and hundreds of articles published in magazines. As The Picture Book Whisperer, they help celebrities write books for children. Ryan lives in Florida.